# The Game
# Theory

URI BRAM

THE GAME THEORY
Kuri Books.

1st Edition.

Text, Images and Cover Design
Copyright © 2013 Uri Bram

ISBN: 1484884078
ISBN-13: 978-1484884072

TO MIKE, DEBRY,

JONATHAN, ANU, ADITYA,

DIANA & JANICE.

# contents

# introduction

A lot of us don't know this about ourselves but everyone is a game theorist. We all employ strategic thinking in our everyday lives: when you get a friend to change your facebook password so you can't log in later; when you pretend you hate Italian food so your buddy is forced to try Thai; or when you're going to a party and want to show up after most of your friends arrive, but most of your friends want to do the same thing. Whenever we change our behaviour in response to other people's choices, and they change their choices in response to ours, we are using game theory whether we like or not.

Perhaps most importantly, we are all private masters of it in the world of dating: we get together in groups with friends to strategise about how we should catch that special someone's attention, and how we should respond to *her* response to our last text message (now don't pull that face at me, I know you know what I'm talking about). You might be wondering whether game theory can really help us in the world of flirting and dating. Fair enough: arguably if economists spent less time making models of social interaction and more time *actually interacting socially* they'd have a more convincing claim to Dating Guru status. Still, the models of strategic interaction that economists have developed in the last century have a lot to teach us about how dating works. These models can help solve puzzles about why the world is as it is, and can even advise us on how we could act differently to make a world we like better.

While I don't want to *promise* that this book will make you more attractive, deliriously happy, and help you find the perfect partner, that's largely for legal reasons. Let's just say that thinking analytically about social life can often be surprisingly productive: when we take a step back and look at our situation more abstractly, we can sometimes find solutions and insights that we wouldn't have managed otherwise. If you take game theory seriously, it really can help you date better. And if you take dating seriously, it can help you become a better game theorist.

# signals

A *flirt*, according to the legendary 18th-Century dictionary-maker Dr. Johnson, was originally a term for a "pert young hussey," then later "a desire of attracting notice,"[1] and though we'd probably phrase it a little differently today you can see where the modern sense came from. The essence of flirtation is that one of you knows something the other doesn't: to flirt is to imply (a whole collection of possible) promises, that you don't necessarily intend to keep, while knowing that your partner doesn't know how sincere you are. In fact, many different dating phenomena revolve around things that the other person knows about herself but that you're still dying to discover. Economists, as it happens, spend a lot of time thinking about just these kinds of situations. Let's get some jargon out the way early on: economists often talk about *asymmetric information*, where one of the parties knows something that the other (initially) doesn't. That seems like a highly useful model for the dating world. Is that cute boy in your lecture nerdily shy or just not into you? Does that girl in the coffee shop always stare at you because she thinks you're cute, or because you look creepily like her ex? Dating is a game in which we try, in various awkward ways, to elicit information from our opposite numbers. And we don't always elicit that information well: lots of mutually beneficial relationships never end up happening because the right information never got through, while others do happen that probably never should have. Ultimately the problem is always the same: your crush knows things about himself that you would like to discover, and he isn't necessarily interested in sharing the information with you.

One common outcome of asymmetric information is something called a *signalling game*. In the game theory model, one of the players gives a signal to try to prove what 'type' she is, while the other tries to learn about the signaller from the signal given. The key insight here is that some signals are more expensive for one type of person than for another, and so 'types' can differentiate themselves by the signals they send. The genius of the model is that it can be worth your while to give a signal even if the signal is very costly for you, just so long as it is *more* costly for your rivals, and so long as it's valuable enough to you that other people know some particular information about you. The classic example is the male peacock: his enormous plumage serves no practical purpose, but it *does* manage to signal a fabulous immune system, since a lesser peacock couldn't possibly afford to waste scarce biological resources on trivial exterior decorating.[2] There are lots of analogues for the flashy peacock on the human dating scene. For example, dressing well is extremely 'costly' in time and energy relative to going outside in sweat-pants. But it is distinctly *less* costly for naturally-stylish people than it is for hard-wired slobs. As such, always being well-dressed can signal various personal traits—good taste, elegance, neatness—that might be attractive to the people we wish to attract.

The clothing example illustrates something important about the basic signalling model: a single action can have both signalling value and inherent value, and talking about "the signalling value of Activity X" doesn't deny that it also has inherent worth. This can be a misunderstanding when economists talk about, for example, the signalling value of college attendance, or the signalling value of charitable giving. To suggest that these activities have signalling value is *not* to say that people are doing them just for show; it's simply to note that the signalling value adds extra appeal to performing a certain activity, over and above its inherent worth. So, for example, dressing well is an inherently rewarding activity: there's an undeniable pleasure to catching a glimpse of yourself in a shiny surface and thinking 'whoah, who's that stunner?" What the signalling model suggests, though, is that people will perform an activity more than they inherently want to if it also provides them signalling value. In the sartorial scene, this seems to be substantiated by the fact that people dress far worse when they're alone in the house and don't think anyone's going to see them.

There's a specific type of signalling game that may be of special interest to us here, in which everyone down a continuum of types is slowly compelled to reveal her private information due to other participants revealing theirs. Basically, if you have private information that you refuse to share, observers will have to make assumptions about the things they can't ascertain. And, in many cases, the observers will assume that what you're hiding is less-than-impressive—if you had something good to reveal, wouldn't you just reveal it? But the logic cascades in such a way that, soon, almost-everyone has an overwhelming incentive to reveal his private information, even if he would ideally prefer to keep it hidden. The thought process goes something like this: If you refuse to show us photos of your new boyfriend then we might assume, to start with, that he is average-looking or even ugly—if he were really cute you'd be much more keen to prove it. But since you know we're going to think like this, if he's simply average-looking you will show us photos anyway, because it's better for you that we know he's average than that we assume he's probably-ugly. But now we assume that if you're not showing us photos he must be anywhere from ugly to *really* ugly, so if he's simply regular-ugly you'll show us a photo to pre-empt our future judgment. Everyone ends up showing photos, unless his or her boyfriend is so terrifying that the photo would be worse than other people's worst imaginings.

This same effect also has serious consequences in the wider world. For example, imagine a law that makes it illegal to ask job-seekers about their criminal record. This might be done in the hope of reintegrating ex-convicts into society, and preventing discrimination against them because of their record. Would such a law work? Well, even if it were illegal for employers to *ask* for information about criminal records, anyone who didn't have such a record would have a pretty glaring incentive to volunteer that information: it might help their job prospects, and there's no way it would hurt. But you see where this is going: now employers would assume that anyone who *didn't* volunteer information actually *did* have a record. Suddenly the ex-cons who only committed minor crimes have an incentive to volunteer that fact, to prevent employers from assuming that their record involves something worse. The cascade continues until everyone voluntarily reveals their criminal record; the law against *demanding* admissions is completely useless, because individual incentives conspire to create full disclosure 'voluntarily.'[3]

Signalling theory can help shed light on one of the most curious, frustrating parts of the dating scene: the 'Hard to Get' strategy, which asserts that seeming unavailable makes you more attractive to the people you'd like to attract. Does the snazzy-dressing model or the show-us-your-photos model explain what's going on with it? Well, partially. On one level, the basic moves of playing hard-to-get are not good signals. Remember that, to be successful, a signal needs to convincingly differentiate you from your lesser rivals. But anybody and everybody is perfectly capable of executing the basic moves of hard-to-get: not-answering-phone-calls, pretending-you-have-plans-tonight, or generally acting aloof and indifferent. In this sense the strategy is too easy to mimic—it's 'cheap' for everyone, and so it shouldn't impress anyone.[4]

On another level, playing hard-to-get correctly is actually pretty hard. The moves themselves may be easy, but performing them is risky: if you act too much like you can afford to lose the person, you might actually end up losing her. Playing hard-to-get is based on trying to imply that you have what, in business, is called an excellent *BATNA*: an excellent Best Alternative to a Negotiated Agreement. By pretending that you're indifferent to your admirer, you are trying to signal that you have great 'outside options,' or at least a lot of confidence that you can snag outside options if necessary. In this sense, the strategy is like the snazzy-dressing problem: it's costly for everyone to play hard-to-get, because there's a genuine risk that you'll lose the person you're interested in, but it's not as costly if you have lots of good fall-backs. It is also like the photo-showing problem, in that there's a continuum of possible actions you can take—do you wait 6 minutes or 60 before replying to that text?—so you're forced to reveal fairly accurately *exactly* how hard-to-get you are. Like in the photo-showing problem, there are lots of people who probably don't want to play hard-to-get at all, but in a world where many others *do* keep playing it, someone who doesn't try to seem at least a *little* unavailable might wrongly be assessed as being irredeemably unattractive.

Your willingness to play hard-to-get, then, signals not a particular aptitude but a particular risk profile—basically, it signals that you don't care what happens with a potential partner and that, somewhat strangely, makes it easier to get what you want. Once again, asymmetric information is the ultimate cause. Here's an analogy: imagine that you're out trying to buy a used car. A good used car can look quite the same as a bad one, because the real difference between them comes from hidden factors (such as how well the previous owner looked after the vehicle) that aren't immediately discernable to a casual observer. If anyone is *too* keen to sell you his car, you should probably be suspicious that he knows something about it you don't.

This was the gist of George Akerlof's seminal 1970 paper, "The market for 'lemons': Quality uncertainty and the market mechanism."[5] Akerlof showed how, under conditions of uncertainty on the buyers' side about the quality of a good, entire markets could deteriorate to the point where no rational seller would be willing to enter the market. Since buyers don't know the true value of a particular car, they have to make offers based on a *market statistic*, that is, a single measure that tells you something useful about the whole population of data: for example, the mean (commonly known as *"the average"*), a single number that tells you what kind of value you can expect from a representative car in the general pool.

Unfortunately for buyers, the sellers *do* know what condition their cars are in, and so have a better gauge of what their particular car is truly worth. What happens if buyers start using the 'population mean' to determine how much they'll offer for a car? Suppose that, in a particular town, there are a hundred-and-one used cars for sale, all superficially indistinguishable but whose true values are in fact $0, $1, $2, up to $100 (that's how much cars cost these days, right?) A little calculation shows that the mean car value is $(0 + 1 + 2 + 3 + ... + 100) / 101$, which handily equals $50. Note that, in one sense, the population mean is a pretty rational price for the buyer to offer: she has a 1/101 chance of getting any particular car, which is a 1/101 chance of getting a car worth $0 and a 1/101 chance of getting a car worth $1 and a 1/101 chance of getting each value of car up to the $100 maximum, so the *expected value* of the car she buys is indeed equal to $(0 + 1 + 2 + 3 + ... + 100) / 101 = $50 = the mean value as calculated above. Since the cars are indistinguishable to her at time of purchase, the rational buyer will (tentatively) offer $50 for any car she looks at.

For the sellers, though, the situation is different. Any seller whose car is worth $51 or more no longer wants to sell; he'd rather keep the $51-car than sell it to someone for $50. The whole dynamic of the market suddenly changes: the cars that are *truly* available have values of $0, $1, ... , $50. But now we have to recalculate the mean: the buyer understands that the expected value of the cars truly available is (0 + 1 + ... + 50) / 51, or $25. You can see where this is going: buyers will now offer $25 for a given car, but sellers won't agree to sell if their car is worth $26 or above. The process repeats, and it's easy to show that we eventually reach zero: the buyer offers $0, and the only person willing to sell is the one whose car is worth exactly that.

The Akerlof model is a gorgeous piece of thinking, and his paper had stunning consequences for the field of economics. But it's clear that it doesn't apply, at least as described here, in the actual market for used cars: obviously there *is* a market for used cars, where cars cost more than $0, so somewhere along the line we are beating out the lemon problem. The model may still hold, in the real world, in a slightly weaker form: there may be a problem of *adverse selection*, where a car on sale is slightly more likely to be low-quality than a car in the population as a whole, but the problem isn't bad enough to destroy the market completely. Why do our used-car markets survive as well as they do?

One of Akerlof's conditions for the existence of a Lemon Market is that sellers have no "credible disclosure technology" — no way to prove to buyers the quality of their cars. But this is not true in the real used-car market. Organisations exist that can validate the quality of a used car before you buy it; the seller can use the "credible disclosure technology" of allowing a mechanic to check out the car before the deal goes through. Another condition for Lemon Markets is a "deficiency of effective public quality assurances, by reputation, regulation, or guarantee." A used car seller can actually offer you a warranty, for example where she agrees to pay all ordinary repair costs for the first few years after the purchase of the car, which is a credible signal of the car's quality because the guarantee is (in expectation) far more costly if the car is low-quality. Even reputation can act as an implicit guarantee, once we talk about large-scale car merchants selling high quantities of vehicles: if a particular seller was notorious for stocking low-quality cars, the news would presumably spread and the seller lose business.

However, there are markets for other goods where the Lemon Market logic truly applies—or, more accurately, because of Lemon Market logic the markets *aren't*. The market for consumer credit in developing countries was once seen as one such case: poor people in poor countries simply couldn't access formal lending (from banks and similar institutions), no matter what interest rate they were willing to pay. Lenders couldn't tell which poor borrowers would be able to repay debts, and it wasn't worth their while to find out, so they outright refused to lend to poor borrowers in general. *Informal* lenders did manage to elicit (perhaps implicit) public guarantees: perhaps, for example, through borrowing conditions like "I will lend you this money, but if you don't pay it back I will break your legs." This elicits a highly effective public guarantee, because (assuming that the threatened leg-breaking is credible) the promise is incredibly costly for a borrower who goes in expecting that she won't be able to pay off her debts. In recent times, the microfinance movement has found a different way to elicit credible guarantees from borrowers: good microfinance institutions lend to groups of borrowers, usually women, and the group is responsible for ensuring that all its members repay their debts. According to the microfinance institutions, the fact that the women live near each other and interact regularly makes it difficult and socially undesirable for any individual to renege on her debt voluntarily, or to take on debt that she doesn't expect to repay.

From what we've seen here, it's probably clear that dating is the ultimate asymmetric information game—there's lots of things *you* know about yourself that *I* don't know, but really want to discover (such as your telephone number. For example. Yeah I'm talking to you, cutie, just scribble it there in the margin. You free on Saturday?). You know such things as whether you're secretly clingy, annoying, overbearing, cheap, or maybe a werewolf; if you seem to be too good for me, but you still want to go out with me, then perhaps there's something you know about yourself that I should beware of. We should all be suspicious, in general, of anyone who is overly keen to date us, like we should be suspicious of anyone who is overly keen to sell us their car—it implies that they think they're getting 'too good a deal.' A person who was genuinely as-good-as-you-could-get would, technically speaking, be *completely indifferent* about dating you. You should have to chase them for a while before they tip your way. In other words: they should be hard-to-get.

Now, before you stop me, I do know dating doesn't work this way. Cars are commodities, and you don't care too much about which specific one you end up with, so long as it meets your needs. But people are people, and sometimes you meet someone and fall head-over-heels for him. You really don't want to date anyone else, so you don't want to act indifferent to whether he likes you. Beyond that, it seems to be true that if you're really, truly besotted with someone, you don't even like her to play hard-to-get with you. In fact, it's pretty much the opposite: if you're truly convinced that you and someone would be perfectly perfect together, you just want her to acknowledge it so the two of you can get together. This raises an interesting point about hard-to-get: the attractive thing about it is somewhere in the *principle* of someone being hard to attain, not in their employment of the strategy itself. There is something peculiar about dating, namely that if someone is considered attractive by lots of *other* people then that in itself is a very attractive thing.[6] This gets to the root of what we've said about hard-to-get: it signals that you have lots of outside options, which is to say, it signals that yet-*other*-people find you attractive too.

Once you realise that this is what hard-to-get is, and the reason that it works, we can start to examine an intriguing possibility: hard-to-get isn't actually attractive, it's just a signal for something that is. As an analogy, imagine that you're new in town and looking for a nice restaurant. You don't *like* big crowds at the places you eat, but a crowd implies that the food is worth waiting for. If you see a long line outside a particular restaurant then you might well wait there because you don't yet have a better way to know where's good. Still, you'd be *even happier* at a place that served great food but didn't keep you waiting. This may seem simple but a lot of people get mixed up about it, and some of those mixed-up people actually try to sell you dating advice. They assume that hard-to-get has *inherent* value: that we like it because we like it. In fact, my best guess is that it only has *signalling* value: we do like people who are hard-to-get, because that implies they're attractive to others, but we'd find the same people even more attractive if they could prove their attractiveness without messing us around for a while. If you can successfully establish that you have great outside options, there is no longer a need to play the game. If a famous actress asked me on a date, I wouldn't worry too much that she couldn't find anyone else.

Now, we can't all make Hollywood movies to prove that we're attractive people. But there's lots of ways you can prove yourself without playing on your unavailability. If you perform in a show or play or concert, where everyone gets to see that everyone else adores you, you massively reduce the usefulness of playing hard-to-get as well. Or if lots of people like you, perhaps because (get ready for this) you're a pleasant, likable human being, and everyone knows that everyone knows that everyone like you, you similarly reduce your need to act unavailable in order to prove your appeal. Especially in environments where reputations are important, and where many of the people you meet will already know each other — on college campuses, for example — an investment in becoming more in-demand can probably be more effective than one in just *seeming* more in-demand. Signalling can easily become an arms race, and waste resources that would be better spent in other ways. The truth is that playing hard-to-get takes a lot more time and energy than is commonly acknowledged, and the same investment could be more productively invested elsewhere—invested in becoming more interesting, charming, and confident.

## The Mystery of Leggings

To move on from hard-to-get, there is another social example of downward-spiralling signalling-wars that is potentially controversial but which I find rather important, so please forgive any offence this might cause. Allow, for a moment, that the fashion for women to wear leggings instead of pants is ugly. I know it's a thing right now, I know that the leggings are supposedly comfy, but the fashion puts more on display than anyone wants to see: if hormonal college-age heterosexual men are telling you that you need to cover your ass more, you really need to wonder if something's gone awry. Now admittedly, some women can just about make it work, but frankly anyone who has a good enough figure to pull off leggings would look *even better* if she wore something, you know, attractive.

Sound familiar? This is exactly where the signalling cascade starts. The women with the best figures will know that they can manage the leggings-look, while none of the other women can. True, the most attractive women would still look better in jeans— better than themselves in leggings, yes, but better than the other women in jeans too (alas, the inequality of physical endowments is just something the rest of us will always have to live with). But a well-cut pair of jeans obscures some of the differences between different figures; there's a reason people look for jeans that sit well on them. By contrast, no matter what anyone tells you, there's no such thing as a pair of leggings that sits well on you: they basically just show off whatever's there to begin with. As such, the wearing of leggings is an opportunity for the most physically-attractive women to increase the 'looks differential' between themselves and others. Even if that comes at the cost of looking worse, it can be a cost worth paying if it helps differentiate them from the competition.

And so we hit the downwards spiral of signals. Once the most attractive women are all wearing leggings, we start to assume that any woman still wearing jeans has something to hide. But then the women with slightly-less-than-perfect figures start wearing leggings too. And again we downgrade our estimate for how good a woman in jeans probably looks—how shall I put this?—underneath those jeans. Pretty soon everyone is wearing leggings, and everyone looks way worse than they need to, but to *not* wear leggings would be as good as confessing a lack of confidence about one's own figure. And you don't want to do that unless you really feel you have no alternative.

Is this really why leggings exist? Well, it truly might be. Yes, as previously noted, various legsponents argue that leggings are simply warm and comfortable, but so are other types of clothing which are decidedly less ugly. And if you insist on wearing leggings, there's no reason why you can't combine them with a shirt that covers your ass (which can actually look o.k, sometimes, if the shirt's right). But if women are putting themselves completely and unnecessarily on display, to basically-everyone's dismay, then there must be a more subtle explanation than either comfort or style.

If you still want something to chew on, there *is* an alternative signalling-based theory of leggings: that women wearing leggings are actually signalling to *each other*, in a kind of Girl Power way, that they're not interested in looking attractive for men. There are obviously times when it's valuable to signal to your gender-mates that they will always be your top priority, that you're not going to abandon them to chase the opposite sex (or romantically-desired members of the same sex). Unfortunately, if you just announce this, nobody will believe you: we've all had too many friends who started a night out proclaiming their unbreakable allegiance to their ladies/bros, and then disappeared as soon as they saw that cutey from the year above across the dance-floor. No, to convincingly promise that you're committed to the group, you need to do something that effectively makes it impossible (or, at least, as difficult as possible) for you to abandon the group in future.

An analogy may be useful here. There is a theory of gang tattoos stating that, in order to make the investment in the training and development of new members, a gang needs to be confident that those same members won't soon abandon the gang for mainstream life. How can you prove to your gang that you'll stay loyal no matter what? Well, getting yourself prominent gang-related tattoos is a long-term, costly gesture that makes it hard or even impossible to pursue non-gang alternatives. The tattoos can make it much less likely that a mainstream employer will hire you, and that very fact makes it more worthwhile for the gang to trust and invest in you in the first place.[7]

From the same perspective, the genius of leggings may be that they allow women to commit to each other that they're not actively chasing men-folk: by making yourself look massively unattractive, you ensure (as much as that is ever possible, which admittedly is "not that much") that guys won't try to get with you. All the verbal promises in the world aren't worth a single bold act that changes your relationship to the outside world in a way that *forces* you to keep those promises. In this case, leggings act as a *credible signal* of disinterest in romantic pursuits: to understand that concept better, we must look in-depth at credible signals.

## Credible Signals

You're already familiar with credible signals from the popular movie, "Every Romantic Comedy Ever Has Exactly The Same Storyline." There's this guy, remember?, and he meets this girl, and they get together, and then he screws up badly, and then... he tries to win her back. But how's he going to show her that he really, truly means it? That she's the only one in the world for him? He has to give a credible signal: he has to do something that just wouldn't be worth it for him *unless* he wanted to spend his life with her.

Imagine there are two types of guys, Really Means It and Really Doesn't, and that The Girl wishes to know what type of guy she is actually dating. Imagine that the benefit that Mr. Really-Means-It gets from a relationship with The

Girl is 10 'points,' and that the benefit Really-Doesn't gets is only 2 points: please don't worry too much about the points thing, I'm *not* saying that relationships can be boiled down to some explicit utility calculation, it's just a succinct shorthand for the complicated way that real relationships work. What's important is that Really-Means-It gets 'more' out of saving the relationship than Really-Doesn't does, which seems obviously true.

Just to start with, if we draw a bar chart for how much each of the men truly like The Girl, the result would look a little something like this:

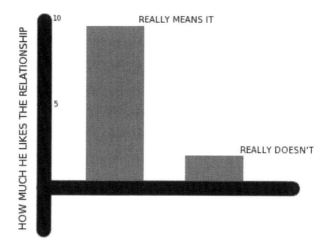

Girl-in-Question is in a bit of a pickle. She knows that her boyfriend is of one of the two types, but she doesn't know which. Finding out may just be important to her because she'd like to be with someone who really, truly means it; knowing his type also has obvious practical implications, because Really-Doesn't is liable to leave her when he meets somebody else he likes more-than-2-much.

Fortunately, there's a solution waiting for our noble heroine: that trusty knight, the Costly Signal. Let's say that there exists some signal of commitment that costs her boyfriend 3 points to perform. This might be something like taking time off work to whisk her away to Paris, or holding hands with her in front of all his bros even though that violates his deeply-held and long-defended bro-code, or overcoming his stereotypical phobia of being vulnerable around other people and truly opening up to her in a charming and highly vulnerable way. The reason this works is that the signal is so costly — 3 whole points! — that it's only worth performing if he values his girl so highly that the relationship is *still* worth it to him after including the expense of the signal. After all, Really-Doesn't would never do something like that: the costly signal would push his overall value of the relationship into the negatives, so he would rather just break up and find someone new than put up with the expense/humiliation/effort of the costly signal.

## AFTER THE SIGNAL:

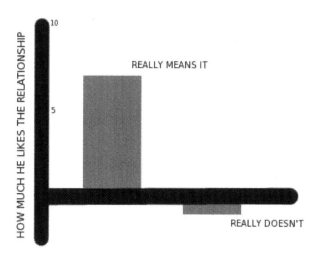

How does this play out in real (movie) life? Well, as previously mentioned, in every good rom-com the male lead must screw up the budding relationship in some cringe-worthy and terrible way, at which point the female lead is inevitably left questioning whether he really cares about her after all. How's he going to prove his devotion? By doing something so emotionally, physically, or psychologically costly that it credibly signals his commitment to her. When Hugh Grant humiliates himself in front of a roomful of strangers at the end of *Notting Hill*, that's a credible signal. When Hugh Grant humiliates himself in front of a churchful of friends at the end of *Four Weddings*, that's a credible signal too. When Hugh Grant doesn't *purposefully* humiliate himself in front of a roomful of strangers at the end of *Love Actually*, that is only because

Love Actually is an ensemble movie and it's Colin Firth's turn to purposefully humiliate himself in front of a restaurant-full of strangers instead.

My favourite example is a movie (which I won't name, to avoid spoiling it) where the male lead screws up and gets kicked out of his lover's house. He almost gives up but gets counselled by another character that "it isn't what you say, much less what you feel— it's what you do to the people you say you love that matters, and it's the only thing that counts."[8] The male lead then sleeps on his lover's doorstep for a week, just sits there and sleeps there in the ice and snow, waiting for her to let him in again. The beauty of the gesture is that it's so incredibly miserable and humiliating — that is, so physically and psychologically costly for him — that she knows he would only do it if he was really, truly serious about her.

"It isn't what you say, much less what you feel," neatly expresses the fact that, in order to be effective, a signal has to be costly enough to prove your type. If a signal isn't costly, it's not a good signal. Verbally apologising is generally not a great signal, if you've screwed up badly enough, because apologies are cheap: they don't really cost you much. Cooking someone dinner is a cheap signal if you like cooking anyway, but an expensive signal if you generally don't cook. Some people make the mistake of thinking how costly a signal would be for them, rather than to the person making it, and then mis-judging other people's signals accordingly. So, for example, if you're dating someone much wealthier than you and find yourself saying "she keeps buying me expensive things. She wouldn't do that if I didn't mean anything to her," you probably need to consider how expensive the gifts are *for her*. Generally speaking, to figure out how costly a signal is to the person giving it, you need to think about what they lack most — be it time, money, or emotional maturity — and how much of that resource they had to expend to give the signal. The more it is, the more that the signal probably means.

But talking about expensive gifts has got me more excited than a wrapping-paper salesman the week before Christmas. And the world of gift-giving has an economic analysis all of its own...

# giving gifts

Gifts, when you think about it, are a funny thing. The idea of taking a stack of perfectly good Money, which another person could use to buy perfectly good Things—things that she knows she wants and enjoys—and instead using that Money to buy her things she potentially-won't enjoy, is pretty odd. From a sheer, materialistic point of view it makes absolutely no sense: she presumably understands herself better than you do, so in the very best case whatever you buy her will (surely) make her only-just-as-happy as the thing she would have bought herself; in the worst case, the thing you buy her will make her much less happy than what she would have bought with the same money, but now you've already bought it and there's nothing she can do.[9]

What's the idea behind gifts, then? There's one argument that the very fact of being given something makes it more valuable, and this is true to an extent: there really is something nice about associating a particular object with the person who gave it to you. But this isn't enough to solve the riddle. For example, why do relatively few people give someone a gift card (or even simple cash) and say "buy yourself something nice with this, and be sure to tell me what it was and think of it as a gift from me?" Or even, "buy yourself something nice, and give it to me, then I'll wrap it and add a card and give it back to you?" That would allow the recipient to select the gift that would make her happiest, but would also ensure she associated it with the person who gave it.[10] No, there's something that people seem to find important about figuring out for themselves what somebody else *would* want, wrapping it up in gift paper, and surprising the recipient. After the previous chapter on signals, you may be thinking to yourself: "might gifts, then, act as a form of signalling?" And indeed they might.

There are a number of signalling-based theories of gifts, some directly contradicting each other. One theory is that a well-chosen gift signals how important the other person is to you, because it shows that you spent a lot of time choosing (and perhaps tracking down) the gift for him. This certainly makes sense for gifts of the type, "remember that jewellery-shop we walked past in Edinburgh, where you pointed out that jade necklace in the window and said how lovely it looked? Well, I found out where it was made, flew out to Okinawa, and convinced the seventy-eight year old monk who makes them to do one with your name on it!" Another obvious option is that gift-selection signals how well you understand a person's tastes and eccentricities: "gah, only you would understand how much I love panda-covered socks!" A more renegade, alternative signalling model of gifts is one in which buying a gift signals how well you know the person by showing how *little* time you spent on finding it. In essence, this model claims that buying a gift for someone is a way of saying, "oh, I *would* have given you cash, but I know and understand you so well that I didn't even have to *think* to know exactly what you'd want."

But here are also numerous non-signalling explanations for the phenomenon of gift-giving. Earlier we noted that the problem with getting someone a gift is that, assuming she knows better than anyone what she herself enjoys, she'd be better off if you gave her the money and she could buy the things she wanted for herself. Looking at this formulation, there are in fact three categories of gifts that you could 'legitimately' give someone even *without* any signalling value to the act of gift-giving. All of them, in some sense, boil down to things that she *couldn't* buy for herself, even if she wanted to.

The first category of gifts is things that the person physically *couldn't* buy herself. Traditionally, this was something like a Gift From a Faraway Country — a hand-carved Egyptian mask that you bought from an old woman in the market at Alexandria, say — which, if you gave your friend the money instead, she would not actually be able to purchase. These kinds of gifts are getting a little less relevant with time, because the number of things from *anywhere* that you can't just purchase on the internet is getting smaller and smaller, but there are still many things that are either impossible or prohibitively expensive to get without going abroad. While it's a known fact of life that, when you travel, it's basically impossible to get round to buying the gifts you intended for the Folks Back Home—first you forget your wallet, then you think you'll find a better price later, and by the time you realise you didn't actually buy anything you're at the tacky airport gift-shop —perhaps this extra nudge from Economic Theory will help you to remember that Little Veda's birthday is coming up, and you really should get him something cool while you're in Freedonia.

This category also includes gifts that the other person couldn't buy for herself because, well, you made them. A hand-made card or a home-cooked dinner can be a good gift not just because it *signals* your willingness to expend time and effort; "an expenditure of your time and effort" might also be something that they'd want to 'buy' for themselves, if they could, but they can't. In a way, this category could subsume the idea that the reason gifts 'work' is because we like to associate an item with a particular person. Even if your friend could easily buy herself the latest Casting Crowns CD, after all, she couldn't buy the latest Casting Crowns CD *from you*. And that's what you're giving her when you give her a gift.

So long as it's strictly understood that this book is in no shape or form encouraging you to break local laws about purchasing for minors, it would be academically dishonest not to mention that a good bottle of liquor for someone who is underage in your jurisdiction is also a way of buying a gift that the person might want, perhaps very much, and yet not be able to buy for herself.

The second category of Gifts That Work is the set of gifts that someone *would* want, if she knew about them, but she doesn't. This could be something like a book (this book?) that is simply perfect for her, and which you know she'd learn a lot from, but which she hasn't read yet. If she hasn't read it then she doesn't know it's perfect for her, and the fact that you do means that (for once) you know what she (would) want better than she knows herself. However, it's important to be aware that this kind of gift expresses a *lot* of confidence in your own understanding of the other person. In some sense this makes it the perfect signalling gift, because if you get it right you've proven that you understand her so wonderfully that you can predict what she wants all by yourself. Empirically, though, most people get their predictions wrong: the number of books and CDs that go unread and unlistened-to, because the giver over-estimated how well she knew the receiver, is (provably) colossal.[11]

The final category of Gifts That Work are the things that a person wants to buy for herself, that she *knows* she wants to buy for herself, that she *can* buy for herself, but that she *won't* buy for herself. This may sound ridiculous but it can be fairly common. One example is ridiculous luxury items: perhaps your friend would secretly like to own a fancy watch, and secretly thinks it's worth the exorbitant price, but still wouldn't buy it for himself if you gave him cash because he wouldn't be able to *rationalise* the fact that he thinks its worth the exorbitant price. By buying him the watch as a gift, you save him from the horrors of guilt and self-justification. And hey, it was *your* idea to buy the watch, and now that you've given it to him it would be rude not to wear it…

The same idea applies to "addictive" goods, like extremely delicious chocolate truffles. A person on a diet might secretly crave chocolate truffles, and would happily buy them with his own money, but he knows he's on a diet so he can't allow himself to. By buying him the truffles, you circúmvent his intellectual diet laws: for some inexplicable reason, things that other people give you don't contain any calories. In some ways, accepting such goods as a gift instead of buying them yourself is just an intellectual cartwheel to avoid personal responsibility, a silly but deliciously-human dodge. There's nothing really wrong with that, and it creates a lot of excellent gift-giving possibilities. But since this book is about game theory, it would be good to mention that there is also a more defensibly rational reason to accept a potentially-addictive good as a gift even while you refuse to buy it for yourself. It would be rational for a person to believe that drinking a bottle of whisky over three or four months is a perfectly healthy, happy activity; it would also be rational for her to believe that, if she allows herself to buy a bottle of whiskey now, she will finish it too fast and impulsively buy another. Making a personal commitment never to buy yourself alcohol can be a useful and rational self-commitment mechanism, in a world where we know our current actions will affect our future desires and where we have preferences over what our future desires will be. "I will never, ever buy alcohol for the house" can be much easier to enforce on yourself than "I will only buy one bottle every 3rd month. Well, maybe every 2nd month, if it's been a hard month. But definitely not more than one bottle a month…"

This self-control mechanism, while useful, seems to force the person never to drink alcohol at all, when in fact she believes that drinking occasionally would make her happier. Voilà: the decision to accept alcohol as a gift, but never to purchase a bottle for herself, allows our heroine to achieve an outcome where she does drink occasionally but is less at risk of escalating her drinking. If you want to thank me for this great advice—well, you can probably guess what to get me.

*Post-Gift Problems*

One thing you may wonder regarding the frequent occurrence of ill-suited gifts is why people don't learn more from their previous gift-giving mistakes. Well, a massive obstacle to giving good gifts is that the feedback you get about whether your *last* gift was appreciated is rarely constructively-critical. This is because of the unique incentive structure that gift-recipients face: even if the recipient actually hates a gift, she will almost certainly feel that she's better off pretending she liked it.

The problem is that once a gift is given it's (generally) over and done with. Being un-enthusiastic about a gift you've received only makes you seem ungrateful and broadly ungracious. It's very, very hard to reject a gift in a way that just makes the other person's gift-choice look bad, without also making yourself look bad in the process. As such, people tend to enthuse heartily about gifts they don't really like, giving rise to stereotypical family-comedies such as the elderly relative who every year buys you a new ugly sweater, which every year you thank him graciously for, which ensures another ugly sweater for the year ahead.[12]

Now, before you start harrumphing me, I will acknowledge that economic theory would predict that gift-giving is exactly the kind of situation where this dilemma should be solvable. This is because gift-giving is an example of an *indefinite horizon game*: you generally expect the gift-giving interaction to be repeated between the exact same parties into the distant future, until or unless some dramatic event occurs. And, in general, a given game can have very different outcomes depending on whether two parties are playing it just once, a finite number of times, or indefinitely. Many deadlocks that cannot be broken in a single-shot or finitely repeated game can be overcome in cases with indefinite repetition.

For example, suppose two merchants are performing a trade where the seller transfers the goods first and the buyer only pays once she's already received them. What's to stop her reneging on the deal and refusing to pay once she already has the goods? Well, in a one-shot game, nothing: if she never plans to see the seller again, she doesn't have to honour their agreement. Knowing this, the seller won't hand over the goods, and the trade simply won't occur in the first place. (In a lighter form, this is one reason why you are especially likely to get fleeced by sellers at a tourist market — they don't expect to see you again, so have no incentive to develop a reputation for honesty or quality). More subtly, the same problem exists in games with *any finite number of repetitions*, if both players know in advance how many turns there will be. How is that so? Imagine that the buyer and seller both know they will interact exactly five times. The seller knows that on the fifth turn the buyer will no longer have an incentive to pay the bill — she can take the goods and run, because she never has to deal with the seller again. As such, the seller might plan that he'll only provide goods on the first four turns and withhold them completely on the fifth. But the buyer can herself imagine this logic, so she plans to stiff the seller on the *fourth* turn instead. The seller sees this coming, and plans to provide goods only on the first *three* turns. And so on, and so on: in the end, all trade becomes impossible.

The only real salvation here is to create a game with *indefinite repetitions*. Suppose, like a normal business, the buyer and seller plan to work together for the foreseeable future. It's possible that one of them will eventually shut down, or move away, or change business, so it's not necessarily true that there will be *infinite* repetitions of the trade. But it *is* true that neither trader knows how long their relationship will last, and that both assume it will continue for the indefinite future. This changes things completely. Without a fixed end point, the buyer always has an incentive to pay her bill for the current round to ensure delivery in the next one. And since the buyer has no incentive to cheat, the seller has no reason to withhold the goods. Indefinite horizons force both players to stay honest for their own future benefit, knowing that their actions today will affect their opportunities tomorrow.[13]

How does all this play out for gift-giving? A simple analysis goes as follows:

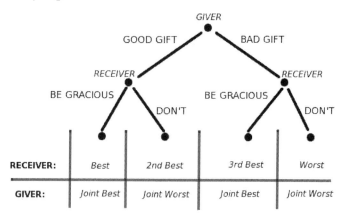

This little picture is something called a *game tree*, and it's one of the economist's favourite doodles; it gives an easy, visual way to understand a situation in which multiple actors have to make decisions which are also influenced by other people's choices. Each of the dots represents a player's turn to make a decision, and the lines branching outwards are the choices the player faces at each juncture: if the giver gives a good gift, and the receiver responds graciously, we find ourselves at the left-most outcome in our diagram above. The text underneath the diagram shows how good the outcome is for each player. Given a choice between two actions on the last turn, the second player will choose the one that secures the better outcome for her from whatever's now available. The first player, on the other hand, has to make his decision while thinking through how the second player will respond to each choice, and figure out how to get the best outcome he can given the choice he expects the second player to make in response to his own.

In this case, the gift giver obviously 'moves first' in the game, by giving the gift, and the receiver responds to this as best she can. The receiver's first preference is to receive a great gift, and to react graciously to it; second-best would be to receive a great gift, but to react ungraciously (because she still gets a great gift that way); her third-best outcome is to receive a *bad* gift and act graciously, because then at least she gets to maintain a good reputation; her worst outcome is to receive a bad gift and be *un*gracious about it, because the gift still sucks and now she's also made her friend feel bad. However, it's important to note that her real choice is how to respond *after* a gift is given. Although she may prefer to receive a good gift ungraciously than a bad gift graciously, this isn't exactly relevant: the gift she gets is (normally) a *fait accompli*, and all that's left is for her to respond as best she can. So we can see that, while the receiver would much prefer to receive a good gift than a bad gift, once the gift is given she will prefer to respond graciously whether it's good or bad.

The giver, on the other hand, has a different set of

incentives. Assume that the receiver is a good enough actress that the giver can't tell whether she's faking her response to the gift (if she's *not* a good enough actress, there's relatively little point in her even trying to pretend she likes the gift). As such, the giver has no preference between giving a good or bad gift *in practice*. Sure, he would much prefer to give a good gift *in theory*, but since he can't actually ascertain whether the gift he gave was good or not, the only thing that really affects his post-gift happiness is how the receiver responds to it. How, then, does he decide between two possible gifts, one of which is (in fact) a good gift and one of which is (in fact) a bad one? Well, we don't know specifically but the answer is basically "at random" or "according to his own personal preferences."

One resulting feature of this game is that the receiver would like to *pre-commit* to responding ungraciously if a gift is bad, because then it will be in the giver's best interest to give a good gift (and achieve his best outcome, which is to receive a gracious response) rather than a bad gift (which would now cause his worst outcome, receiving an ungracious response). The problem in a one-shot game is that the receiver has no way to commit credibly that she will respond ungraciously to a bad gift: once the gift is actually given, her incentives make her want to respond graciously whether the gift is good or bad. This is the situation that pertains, for example, when dealing with long-lost relatives who show up only for weddings or bat mitzvahs: they will probably get you a gift you don't like, but since you only see them every-other decade, it's not worth not-pretending that you simply love what they got you.

Most gift-giving situations, though, would seem to be exactly the type of indefinite-horizon games we spoke of early, and which should be able to offer an escape from disappointing gifts: most gift-receivers expect to have gift-interactions with most of their gift-givers a few times each year for as long as they both shall live, so if a receiver reacts badly to a bad gift now she might change the giver's behaviour in future interactions. This *should* create an incentive for her to risk a bit of awkwardness now in order to ensure better outcomes in future.[14]

Unfortunately, this chapter is going to end with a cop out: I don't have an explanation for why so many people continue to receive (literal or metaphorical) Ugly Sweaters from particular relatives year after year. A morose explanation is that perhaps people are most accepting of Ugly Sweater-type gifts from relatives who are very elderly and who, to put it horribly euphemistically, they foresee a relatively short 'game horizon' with.[15] Another explanation is that, since gifts are such a vanishingly small part of your total yearly interaction with your regular gift-givers, 'forcing' better gift-selection just isn't worth it because of negative effects on other elements of your relationship with them.

Truthfully, though, neither of these explanations is completely satisfying. And this reflects one of the big challenges of economic analysis, and of analysing complex systems in general: one thing always affects another, and the consequences you're looking for may have wriggled to another part of the system or been swamped completely by some other factor. As such, the outcomes we see might not be the ones that a cursory application of the model would predict, even if the model itself is correct (though not complete). If you have a better answer for why the Ugly Sweater problem persists, I'm sure a lot of people (and their sweater-filled closets) would love to hear from you.

# promiscuity

The following discussion is not opinion, it's logic. Sure, authors normally say that when they're about to tell you their opinion, but on this occasion it's literally so: what I'm about to write is not just true but *necessarily* true. At this point you'll be asking yourself, "if what's coming up is so glaringly right, what's the need for such a ridiculously over-wrought pre-amble?" Because it's also relatively counter-intuitive, and gets a lot of people annoyed when you mention it. I'm going to sit way back from my laptop while I type this, just in case anyone lashes out.

The question-in-question is this: who is more (heterosexually) promiscuous, men or women? Let's define promiscuity (just for the moment) as average number of sexual partners in a lifetime. Take a minute to think about that: think about all the men you know, and think about all the women, and then decide whether you think the men or the women have had more sexual partners on average. Now forget everything you've just thought about, because it's irrelevant to the question I posed: the answer is that men and women, overall, must have (so-close-to-exactly that the difference isn't worth worrying about) an equal number of heterosexual partners on average.[16]

If your initial response is "that *can't* be true, men just *obviously* have more partners than women" then the argument in this chapter should (hopefully) convince you otherwise. On the other hand, if your initial response is "maybe men and women overall have equal numbers of partners on average, but the average isn't equal among my peers" (or among college kids, or among hipsters, or some other relevant demographic) then you could certainly be right: there's no mathematical reason why, within a certain demographic or social group, there can't be an imbalance in the average number of sexual partners. And if your initial response is "well, mean average isn't the interesting thing — when I say 'promiscuity' I'm talking about distributions, and the *distribution* of sexual partners between men and women could certainly be different" then you're right too. All I can say to these readers is 'sit tight;' we'll return to these issues briefly at the end of the chapter. Our focus here, though, will be the overall average number of heterosexual partners for men and women. There are many other interesting questions to ask about promiscuity, but this is the one that can be answered definitively using theory alone. And this being a book on theory, we'll leave the hard empirical slog of answering other questions for some other book (you're welcome, Other Book).

Let's return to our central claim: for men and women overall, the average number of lifetime sexual partners must be equal. This answer is not based on particular observations of particular men and women, and thinking about particular men and women can only possibly mislead you. The answer doesn't depend on what happens in survey data, so any surveys that contradict it are showing something about what people *say* but not about what they *do*. The truth follows simply and inevitably from the logic of graph theory. This observation, in common with almost every other anecdote in popular social-science books, was already discussed decades ago by the economist Thomas Schelling. In his "Micromotives and Macrobehavior,"[17] Schelling highlights an entire class of interactions where the average number of X's must, when you really think about it, necessarily equal the average number of Y's. For example: which is higher?, the average number of phone calls made or the average number of calls received by each person each year? In the end they must be exactly equal, so long as we consistently define "calling" and "being called," because each message is sent once and received once. Did the average NBA team score more points or have more scored against it during the last season? Again, the average must be identical so long as we define the problem in a reasonable and consistent manner.

As a less-fun example, economists will tell you that there are two ways to calculate GDP-per-capita (that is, national income per head): the Expenditure Method (which is all the money spent on goods and services) and the Income Method (which is all the money earned by people), and that the two are exactly (but exactly) equal. It can be hard to accurately count all the money changing hands in an economy, so maybe we can't *track* the way that national income and national expenditure work out to be the same. But at the end of the day, they must be: every dollar spent by one person (expenditure) is earned by somebody else (income), so average expenditure and average income must be equal.

What do all these relationships have in common? Well, they all involve people or groups interacting with each other. In fine economic tradition, we'll call these actors "actors." In any given interaction, each actor can perform only one of two distinct roles — making or receiving a call, paying for a service or getting paid for it — so, even if (say) the same people both make and receive calls over time, we say that there are two "sets" of actors, "call makers" and "call receivers." In the case of the phone-calls, the exact same actors are being counted once in the first set and once in the second set; in the case of (heterosexual) promiscuity, men and women are the two distinct sets. In every case (that fits this model) there are an exactly-equal number of actors in each set, and each interaction links exactly one actor in the first set to exactly one actor in the second.[18] So long as these conditions hold, the average number of interactions from one 'side' will automatically be equal to the average number from the other side. To return to our chapter-theme, this model sheds light on the world of promiscuity. So long as we define sexual relationships in a sensible way — such that if some act 'counts' for one partner it must also count for the other — it is necessarily true that the average (heterosexual) promiscuity of men and women must be equal.

One condition that follows from those above is that we must be looking at a "closed" population; all interactions occur between actors in the two sets, not with actors in additional sets. If we have two neighbouring countries whose populations mix regularly then it may be the case that *within one country* men have more sexual partners on average than women, but only if in the other country women have more sexual partners on average than men. Taking the two countries together, the average promiscuity has to be equal. Similarly, it could be true that (say) college-age women are more promiscuous than college-age men, but only if post-college men are more promiscuous than post-college women. Once we take the system as a whole, the average promiscuity must be equal. Of course, this caveat would technically mean that male and female promiscuity within such a system as "The United States" need not be equal, since some Americans do sleep with non-Americans. However, unless you think that a fairly significant number of Americans are being internationally promiscuous, *and* that there is a stark male-to-female difference in this international promiscuity, the international cases won't matter much to the national averages.[19]

Now, the fact that *mean average* promiscuity between

men and women is necessarily identical does not mean that the *distribution* has to be similar: the distributions of the number of sexual partners could be massively different. To illustrate, imagine a hypothetical population of four men and four women: an average of one sexual partner per person could be achieved through:

- four monogamous couples;
- two women both sleeping with the same two men, while two other men and two other women sleep with nobody;
- one man who sleeps with all four women, while three other men don't sleep with anybody — or vice versa, one woman who sleeps with all four men, while three women sleep with nobody;
- etc., etc., etc. To be more precise: there are eleven possible "patterns" in this eight-person game *just* for cases with an average of one partner per person, *and* assuming that it doesn't matter who specifically is sleeping with who (which, to the people involved, it probably does).

The following diagrams illustrate some of these "patterns" of promiscuity, all leading to an average of one partner per person. The two sides of the diagrams are purposefully left unlabelled to illustrate that the problem is symmetrical: either side could represent either men or women.

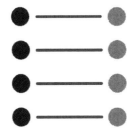

LEFT HAND SIDE MEAN:
(1 + 1 + 1 + 1) / 4 = **1**
RIGHT HAND SIDE MEAN:
(1 + 1 + 1 + 1) / 4 = **1**

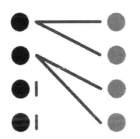

LHS MEAN: (2 + 2 + 0 + 0) / 4 = **1**
RHS MEAN: (1 + 1 + 1 + 1) / 4 = **1**

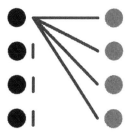

LHS MEAN: (4 + 0 + 0 + 0) / 4 = **1**
RHS MEAN: (1 + 1 + 1 + 1) / 4 = **1**

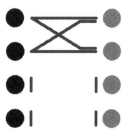

LHS MEAN: (2 + 2 + 0 + 0) / 4 = **1**
RHS MEAN: (2 + 2 + 0 + 0) / 4 = **1**

For the maths to work, it's important to remember that people who are having no sex are still people (yes, shockingly) and so to include the "0"s when doing the calculation.

None of these arguments apply to homosexual promiscuity. There is no reason to think that male homosexuals have the same average number of partners as female homosexuals; these are two closed and separate systems that are completely independent from each other. The averages could be the same, or similar, or completely different; they could both be high, or both be low, or one high and one low (at the extreme, one could be zero and the other could be n-1, where $n$ is the size of the relevant population). The point is that, while the average heterosexual promiscuity of men and women is intrinsically linked, the average homosexual promiscuity of men and women has no inherent relationship whatsoever. Two possibilities are shown below, again where either colour of dots could represent either men or women:

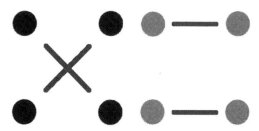

LHS MEAN: (1 + 1 + 1 + 1) / 4 = **1**
RHS MEAN: (1 + 1 + 1 + 1) / 4 = **1**

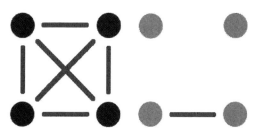

LHS MEAN: (3 + 3 + 3 + 3) / 4 = **3**
RHS MEAN: (1 + 1 + 0 + 0) / 4 = **½**

Now let's return to the average number of heterosexual partners for men and women, which we showed necessarily had to be equal. It's important to remember that the whole equal-averages thing isn't obvious until you know it. We can see that from newspaper headlines such as "In the age of promiscuity, women have more sexual partners than men,"[20] a statement that (as written in the headline) is as mathematically moronic as "in the age of the iPhone, 3 equals 5." At the same time, headlines such as "Men are no more promiscuous than women, survey finds" (subhead: "The long standing belief that men are promiscuous and women are choosy is a myth, claim psychologists,")[21] are equally ill-formed, even if they happen to arrive at (roughly) the right conclusion. A survey *couldn't* prove that men, overall, are no more promiscuous than women on average (in the sense of 'promiscuous' being used in these newspaper headlines), any more than a survey could 'prove' what $2 + 2$ equals. Of course, the subhead hints at a possible cause for all the confusion: some people assume that heterosexual men are more promiscuous than heterosexual women because they beleive that the men are more *interested* in sex than the women. This could be true, or it could be false, there's no logical necessity either way.

One of the amusing things about this particular proof is that you can sketch it for people pretty easily on a napkin, making it a lot of fun to argue about with people at dinner (it's one of the rare arguments where you might even convince your opponent, because the logic is hard to dispute once you see it clearly). It also has some pretty clear real-life consequences: if you previously thought that the other sex is less (more) promiscuous than yours overall, you now need to raise (lower) your estimate accordingly. In various ways that I'll leave to your own understanding, how we interact with the opposite sex, and what we believe about our own sex, is influenced by how promiscuous we think the two sexes are.

On the other hand, I don't want to over-state the scope of this promiscuity argument: some of your dinner-party companions will reply "your logic is great, but you're answering the wrong question."[22] And they're certainly right that graph-theory argument doesn't come close to covering all the interesting questions about promiscuity. For example, one interesting question is average numbers of sexual partners among a particular demographic group: do college men or college women have more sexual partners, on average? What does that tell us about social norms (and social taboos)? Many people who discuss promiscuity are probably thinking about their peers specifically, and (as previously noted) there is no mathematical reason why average number of heterosexual partners needs to be equal among a specific demographic group. We'd need to get empirical data from real people to answer that question, something that is well outside the scope of this book. One insight that this chapter's promiscuity model can give us here, though, is the understanding that if one sex has more heterosexual partners within a certain demographic then it must be 'balanced' somewhere else in the system: if under-25 women have more heterosexual partners than under-25 men, the opposite must be true for over-25 women and men.

Another interesting question about promiscuity concerns distributions. There is no mathematically necessary reason why the *distribution* of heterosexual partners between men and women should be in any way similar: as we showed in the graphs above, there are many different "pairs" of distributions that can go together, including highly equal ones (where all men and all women have the same number of heterosexual partners) and very unequal ones (where one sex has a few very promiscuous people and many un-promiscuous people, while the other sex has very many slightly promiscuous people). Unfortunately, the empirical evidence about this question is again outside the scope of this book. But while theory alone can't tell us which distribution applies to each sex in the real world, it *can* tell us some basic conditions that *have* to be met.

As such, it's interesting to ask people who instinctively think that, say, men are more promiscuous than women exactly what they mean. Do they mean that the most promiscuous men have had many more partners than the most promiscuous women (but that then, necessarily, there are many less-promiscuous women with more sexual partners than the less-promiscuous men)? Or perhaps the opposite, that many women have had no or few sexual partners while equally-many men have had multiple sexual partners (but that then, necessarily, there are a few especially-promiscuous women with very many sexual partners)? It's not clear that either of these options aligns very well with our cultural stereotypes about promiscuity, which might mean we need to re-consider some of our lazier folk-theories. This is the great contribution that the graph theory argument can give us in this debate: even when it can't provide the whole answer, it can narrow down the options and force us to forge more accurate theories.

# hang-ups

Long, romantic phone conversations with your guy/ gal are one of the most exciting parts of a budding young relationship: those long hours when, in the immortal words of Taylor Swift, "we're on the phone and you talk real slow/ 'cause it's late and your momma don't know."[23] The problem with those Long Romantic Phonecalls is that they can last (almost) *forever*. Long after you both stopped enjoying yourself, long after you both remembered you had other stuff to do, you find yourself still on the line. Why? Because neither side wants to hang up first. *Aw, babe, you hang up first.* **No you hang up first**. *I love you.* **I love you more**. *Um.* **Well**. *What was that thing you were telling me earlier?* **Oh, yeah, it was nothing. Well...**

In many ways, this situation poses something of a mystery. Why would two rational people waste significant chunks of time doing something that neither of them wants to do? Obviously the phone conversation *as a whole* makes both of them happy, but standard economic logic would dictate that once the 'marginal benefit' of the call (the additional benefit from spending an extra minute on it) gets swamped by the 'marginal cost' — which is to say, once an additional minute of time on the phone is actually subtracting from your enjoyment of the world, rather than adding to it — you should both be able to agree to finish the call. Unfortunately, in the strategic interaction of a phone conversation, things aren't quite that simple.

Economists in fact have a model of a very similar game — it's called the Dollar Auction, first developed by

Martin Shubik.[24i] Here's the idea: the Auctioneer waves a dollar bill in the air, and asks if anyone wants to buy it. The starting bid is 5¢, which sure sounds like a bargain. The only rule is that *both* the winner and the runner-up have to pay their final bid, and of course the winner gets to keep the dollar. As it turns out (in the words of Shubik), "[t]he game is simplicity itself and is usually highly profitable to its promoter ... a large crowd is desirable, [and] experience has indicated that the best time is during a party when spirits are high and the propensity to calculate does not settle in until at least two bids have been made."[24ii]

Here's how it works: suppose Anna has started the bidding at 5¢, and Billy has jumped in at 10¢. Anna now has a choice: if she lets things stand then, as the runner up, she will lose 5¢ and win nothing; if she instead bids 15¢ then she stands to win the dollar, pay her 15¢, and gain 85¢ overall. But of course, once Anna bids, an almost-identical argument applies for Billy: if he stays where he is then he'll lose 10¢, but if he instead bids 20¢ then he gets the chance to gain 80¢ overall. Things get really funny when we reach the $1 mark. Suppose Anna's last bid was 95¢, and Billy has gone ahead and bid $1. Anna has two choices now· drop out of the game, and lose 95¢ flat, or bid $1.05, and stand to lose only 5¢. The absurdness of bidding $1.05 to win a $1 bill no longer matters; the important thing is to cut your losses. Shubik says that "[a] total of payments between three and five dollars is not uncommon."[24iii]

Shubik describes the "static game theory analysis" for this problem — that is, roughly, the analysis when viewing Anna and Billy's game as an isolated incident, and avoiding awkward questions about why either of them got involved in the first place — as "trivial," in the mathematical sense meaning something like 'following pretty inevitably from things we already know.'[25] In the previous paragraph we saw that it is indeed quite trivial to go from Anna's 5¢ bet and Billy's 10¢ bet to a situation where they're each willing to bid over a dollar to buy a dollar. The problem is that the static analysis is very clearly missing something. In economics generally, many problems that can be solved relatively easily as static games become pitiless beasts when we try to solve them *dynamically*: that is, when we try to give a solution that takes into account how people respond to the game after they've played it once already, and why anyone would get involved in the game once they'd thought through what will happen at the end of it.

What exactly is wrong with the static analysis of the Dollar Auction? The logic at each stage seems to rely on the bidders not really looking ahead: once Billy bids 10¢, Anna should really be thinking "I could bid 15¢, but then he'll bid 20¢, and I'll bid 25¢, and soon I'll be losing money anyway, so I might as well cut my losses now and pay the measly 5¢." The fact that, in real-life implementations of the game, people eventually do stop bidding implies that they eventually figure this out — in the post-$1 world, it is only rational to keep bidding upwards if you think that you are able to outlast your opponent *and* that your opponent will quit within 95¢ of the current price. But more importantly, in a dynamic analysis of the Dollar Auction setup, both players should actually see the whole mess unfolding from the beginning and never even enter the game in the first place—it's only going to end in tears. The fact that the game ever gets started therefore relies on a kind of initial irrationality.

Putting those concerns aside, Shubik notes that the game relatively rarely applies in real life. "In bargaining between bureaucracies or nations ... [l]arge time lags are present in the system. Furthermore, statements and explicit displays of intent concerning future behavior can be, and are, made."* These two factors prevent Dollar Auction-style escalation from taking place. But one real-life "negotiation" which *does* seem equivalent is the You Hang Up First game. Since neither side wants to be the first to hang up, we could say that the two parties bid for the "not-hanging-up prize" (instead of bidding for a dollar). Assume that whoever doesn't-hang-up wins 100 "Romance Points" for *not* being the one to acknowledge that, whatever you tell each other, you don't literally want to spend all day on the phone together. Once you are both bored of talking, each of you incurs a cost of 5 Points for every 'conversational move' made during which neither of you ends the conversation. Assume that the conversation consists of alternating turns (this is just for simplicity) and assume, for the moment, that both partners get bored of the conversation at exactly the same time.

We can see that the outcome is the same as the Dollar Auction. Suppose Anna is talking at the exact moment that both partners have had enough of the conversation. She could hang up right now and let Billy get the 100-point not-hanging-up bonus, or she could keep talking and lose 5 points but then potentially win 100 next 'move' when Billy hangs up instead. It feels like a no-brainer. Then, on Billy's go, he can either let Anna win the 100 points or he can accept the 10-point-loss and win 100 points back when Anna hangs up. You can see where this is going: a little while later they've both lost 100 points just from boredom, and both of them wish that they'd hung up as soon as the conversation got stale. But now that they've *already* spent so much time hoping the other will be first to hang up, and since it costs so little to wait *just one more turn*, the conversation keeps going just a little bit longer. And going, and going — *Aw, babe, you hang up first*. **No you hang up first** — for the rest of time.

Is there a solution? Like most things: sort of. In theory, one solution is to set a (real, or fake) deadline for the conversation to end: **hello?** *hey sweetie* **ahhh it's so**

**good to hear your voice** *is now good?* **yeah!, it's great. BUT, I do have to be at this** *thing* **in an hour, I hope that's o.k....**

Of course, the great benefit of an entirely fake deadline is that you can later cancel it. *Oh, y'know, I think I'll just skip that... thing. Yeah, they'll be pissed. But I'd rather be talking to you.* Since you probably don't want to just make stuff up, it's more likely that you'll use a "soft" deadline— *Yeah, I have to get to dinner before 8 or the dining hall closes.* In these situations, your willingness to incur a penalty for still being on the phone is a credible signal of your affection for your partner—love that is worth missing dinner for is precious indeed. But then, necessarily, a display of *un*willingness to incur the penalty also sends a signal. You therefore become trapped in the exact same Dollar Auction problem as before: you both want to end the conversation so you can get to dinner, but neither of you wants to be the one to say it, and the conversation keeps rolling.

The pre-emptive deadline strategy *can* still be useful, however, if you and your partner are relatively realistic people: it can act as a kind of negotiated agreement to exit the auction and "split" the reward-points at whatever time you both run out of things to say to each other. Why exactly two people would be rational enough to be able to enforce such an agreement, but not rational enough to just be able to say *hey, it's been great chatting with you, talk again tomorrow?* I can't exactly explain. I *will* say that the situation still arises, rational or otherwise. Whether you know it or not, sometimes your partner doesn't want to keep the conversation going any more than you do—he may just be pretending because he thinks *you* want to, even while you're faking enthusiasm only because he is. So putting out feelers about mutually releasing yourselves from the conversation could be a good option.

This entire discussion has assumed, of course, that

we've reached a situation where both parties are tired of the call and would like to end it, if they could. If your problem is instead that you get tired of phonecalls before your partner does, that's something of a harder problem. Of course, pre-emptively pretending that you have an unbreakable deadline could still work; however, we're now moving away from How to Use Game Theory towards How To Lie to People Nicely. This isn't the book for that, though I'm sure there's one out there somewhere.

# coda

Well, that's that. Through the course of this book we've discovered magical things about the deeply connected worlds of dating and game theory.

We began with *signalling games*, which can help explain why someone might feel pressured to show us photos of her boyfriend even if she doesn't want to. We've seen how signalling could explain the frustrating *hard to get* strategy, the enduring *mystery of leggings*, and the *credible signals* that show their signally faces by the end of every romantic comedy.

In the world of *gift-giving* we saw why the best kinds of gifts might be the ones that a person couldn't buy for herself, whether because they're not physically available to her, because she doesn't yet know about them, or because she can't psychologically bring herself to buy them. After that, we asked why some people keep giving you terrible, terrible presents.

Next we looked at *promiscuity*, and discovered a little piece of graph theory proving that men and women must have the same number of lifetime sexual partners on average. We also discovered that there are harder questions about promiscuity that graph theory can't answer, but that it can give us little clues for.

Finally, we saw how the game theoretic analysis of the Dollar Auction can help to explain why two halves of a couple both refuse to *hang up the phone first*, and suggested some solutions for this touching but troubling problem.

And that brings us to the coda, which it would be

silly to summarise since you're reading it right now. What more is there to say about the wonderful worlds of game theory and dating? Actually there's a world-ful of additional wonder out there — check out the end of the Sources section for some recommended reading. But for now, just remember: taking game theory seriously can truly help you date better, and taking dating seriously can truly improve your game-theoretical prowess. So take this book in one hand and that special someone in the other, and play the dating game with a little help from game theory.

# sources

In this book, I have made peace with the fact that 'proper' old-school references are now less useful than simple Googling directions. The references below do not follow any consistent style-guide, but instead contain whatever information will help you find that particular source most easily.

## signals

1. FLIRT: Check out the excellent "A Dictionary of the English Language; in which the words are deduced from their originals; and illustrated in their different significations, by examples from the best writers," by Samuel Johnson LL.D. Available in its entirety through Google Books, and a search for "pert young hussey" (in Vol. II) will bring you to the right page (and greatly improve your search history).

2. PEACOCKS: See "Mate Selection—A Selection for a Handicap," by Amotz Zahavi, in the Journal of Theoretical Biology, 1975. Available through Google Scholar and potentially for free through regular-Google if you search 'Zahavi Mate Selection' (no quotemarks).

3. CRIMINAL RECORDS: While I know that I didn't originate this example, I unfortunately can't find sources for who did; for some reason I thought it was Alex Tabarrok, but can't find anything confirming that online.

If you happen to know, please do get in touch.

4. HARD TO GET: The insight that basic hard-to-get is too easy-to-mimic, and proper hard-to-get is hard-to-get-right, is credited to "The economics of seduction?," by Tyler Cowen, on MarginalRevolution.com, 2005.

5. LEMONS: See "The market for "lemons": Quality uncertainty and the market mechanism," by George Akerlof, The Quarterly Journal of Economics, 1970. Available through Google Scholar, and potentially for free through Google if you search 'the market for lemons akerlof pdf' (no quotemarks).

The Wikipedia article called 'The Market for Lemons' is also good and clear, if you'd like to learn more.

6. ATTRACTIVENESS IS ATTRACTIVE: To get technical, I would probably argue that romantic partners are (at least in part) association goods. See "A Theory of Association: Social Status, Prices and Markets," by Kaushik Basu, Oxford Economic Papers, 1989. Available through Google Scholar, and potentially for free through Google if you search "A Theory of Association" inside quotemarks.

7. TATTOOS: I don't know who originated this theory, but an excellent description and discussion is available at "Gang Tattoos: Signs of Belonging and the Transience of Signs," by Lina Goldberg, linagoldberg.com/gangtattoos.

8. NOT WHAT YOU SAY: To find the movie, google the phrase "What you feel only matters to you"

## giving gifts

9. JUST AS HAPPY: An astute reviewer points out the analysis in this chapter only applies if you are buying a gift in order to make someone happy—not to shame her, or educate her, or something else. It could be perfectly rational (though not very nice) to get someone a gift that she wouldn't have bought herself if your gift has one of these alternative intentions.

10. MONEY AND GIFTS: The people who, in my completely unscientific experience, tend to actually do this most often are Grandparents. There are two ways to view the Grandparently willingness to give cash instead of gifts: 1) Grandparents so obviously love you and care about you that they no longer need to signal their care and attentiveness; they can get away with giving cash because you'd never doubt how much they love you anyway; 2) Grandparents, being unusually wise and ready to admit that they're not really sure what Young People Like These Days, are more-than-usually willing to acknowledge that they don't know what kind of gift you'd enjoy—their gift of cash does signal that they don't know what you want, they're just special in their willingness to admit that.

In separate news, much of this chapter is inspired by things read somewhere on the internet, but unfortunately I can't find many of the proper attributions. If you feel that some idea in this chapter should be credited to a particular author, please do get in touch.

11. WASTED GIFTS: See "The Deadweight Loss of Christmas," by Joel Waldfogel, American Economic Review, 1993. Available through Google Scholar, and potentially for free through Google if you search 'joel waldfogel deadweight loss' (no quotemarks).

12. UGLY SWEATERS AND BAD SERVICE: To some extent, a similar problem exists in restaurants: when the waiter comes round to ask "how is everything?," a decent number of customers feel that to complain about the meal would make them look bad in front of the waiter and not achieve anything constructive (maybe the dish would be taken back and replaced, but then there's a worry about what exactly goes into the replacement). So they smile and say everything's wonderful, even when it isn't, and consequently the restaurant doesn't receive the feedback it ought to about the quality of its offerings.

13. HORIZONS: The indefinite horizon doesn't necessarily have to be between the buyer and seller directly. One reason that a shop-keeper may decide not to fleece you, even if you both expect to interact with each other only once, is that you both have an indefinite-horizon relationship with the government, police, and regulatory agencies in the relevant jurisdiction, and know that the other party could punish you through these agencies if you act improperly. On the other hand, this is why trade is harder in places without meaningful governance and rule of law.

14. AWKWARDNESS: The delightful I. suggests that by acknowledging the gift-giver's need to give you a good gift, you may be able to achieve better gifts in future without offending the giver: "[for example,] "thank you, I appreciate you giving me a warm sweater, and I would have loved it even more if it was an all blue sweater" … is more likely to result in a better gift next time than "You have terrible fashion sense, I hate this.""

15. MOROSE: The wonderfully insightful M. suggests a less-morbid explanation: "perhaps the thought is not "Oh well, he won't be around to give me ugly sweaters for

long," but rather "Gee, if his taste is so poor that he thought this ugly sweater was a good idea, he might give me something even worse if my lack of gratitude prompts him to choose a different kind of gift next time.""

## promiscuity

16. PROMISCUITY: Alright, alright, but if you insist: the lone caveat here is that this *would* be 100% true if there were *exactly* the same number of men and women in a society. In fact, there are slightly more women than men in ordinary human populations: for example, at the time of writing, 50.8% of Americans are female. The literally true statement is that if there are $m$ males in a population and $f$ females then $mX_m = fX_f$, where $X_i$ is the average number of sexual partners each person of that gender has. If $f =1.016m$, as in the American case, then $X_m = 1.016X_f$, i.e. women will only have 98.4% as many sexual partners as men. But don't try to tell me that anyone says "men are more promiscuous" and really means "1.016 times more promiscuous, to be precise."

This entire section is so far from being original that I don't even know where to start – it's long been a staple of popular economics books and newspapers columns. I think I've read about it in a Steven Landsburg book, and also in a piece by John Allen Paulos, and possibly also a column by Tim Harford... just so nobody thinks I'm claiming credit here.

17. SCHELLING: "Micromotives and Macrobehavior," by Thomas Schelling, rereleased in 2006. Available on Amazon for about $12. Seriously, seriously, if you only do one thing I ask you in life, get this book– you'll thank me for it. Well, you *should* thank me for it, I don't know how good your manners are.

18. SETS AND SETSABILITY: For the graph-theoretically inclined – and this will not be clear unless you are already familiar with graph theory, in which case it may be redundant – the formal statements would look like this:

*"actors can perform only one of two distinct roles"* i.e. the vertices of G can be divided into two disjoint sets, $U$ and $V$. *"each interaction links exactly one actor in the first set to exactly one actor in the second,"* i.e. each edge connects exactly two vertices (i.e. the graph is simple/has no loops), and every edge connects a vertex $u$ in $U$ to a vertex $v$ in $V$.

These provide the conditions for a bipartite graph, namely, a graph G whose vertices can be divided into two disjoint sets, $U$ and $V$, such that every edge $e$ in G connects a vertex $u$ in $U$ to a vertex $v$ in $V$.

*"there are an exactly-equal number of actors in each set."* i.e. there are an equal number of vertices in $U$ and in $V$.

This provides the condition for a bipartite graph to be balanced.

From there it's pretty simple: the sum of the degrees of all vertices $u$ in $U$ must equal the sum of the degrees of all the vertices $v$ in $V$, because the graph is bipartite. We know that $|U| = |V|$ because the graph is balanced. Therefore, the average degree of the vertices $u$ in $U$
= the average degree of the vertices $v$ in $V$
= (the sum of the degrees of the vertices $v$ in $V$) / ($|V|$)
= (the sum of the degrees of the vertices $u$ in $U$) / ($|U|$).
QED, kids.

19. NATIONAL AVERAGES: There are a few countries which may have truly stark gender-promiscuity differences,

despite having relatively equal male-female ratios: countries with particularly large sex-tourism industries come to mind, though I have not verified this at all.

20. HEADLINE ILLOGIC 1: "In the age of promiscuity, women have more sexual partners than men," by Paul Sims, The Mail, 9 December 2008. Available through Google if you search "women promiscuity paul sims" (no quotemarks).

The article goes on to make specific claims about subgroups (e.g., "By the age of 21 [women] have had sex with an average of nine lovers – two more than their male partner") which could, theoretically, be true, but the title itself cannot. But don't get me wrong: just because it's not necessarily false, doesn't mean I believe that the under-21 claim is true either. Given that the 'study' cited was really a survey for a women's magazine, doesn't say anything about the sampling method, doesn't say how many men were surveyed (if any – the wording leaves open the ridiculous possibility that the authors simply asked women how many sexual partners their partner had had...) the sensible guess is probably that the entire 'study' is utterly meaningless. Regardless, a logically-impossible headline should not be publishable under any circumstances.

The Telegraph reported the exact same story under the buck-passing headline, "Young women 'have more sexual partners' than men," by Martin Beckford, 8 December 2008. Available through Google if you search "sexual partners martin beckford" (no quotemarks).

21. HEADLINE ILLOGIC 2: "Men are no more promiscuous than women, survey finds," by Richard Alleyne, The Telegraph, 24 April 2009. Available through Google if you search "men promiscuous richard

alleyne" (no quotemarks).

22. THE WRONG QUESTION: This paragraph, and many others in this chapter, are thanks to insights from the brilliant J., a man I don't get nearly enough dinner-parties with.

**hang ups**

23. TAYLOR SWIFT: "Our Song," by Taylor Swift, I'm sure you can find it on the internet. The completely unnecessary use of this reference is dedicated to the beautiful K.

24. SHUBIK: "The Dollar Auction Game: A Paradox in Noncooperative Behavior and Escalation," by Martin Shubik, Journal of Conflict Resolution, 1971. Available through Google Scholar, and potentially for free through Google if you search 'martin shubik dollar auction' (no quotemarks).

The following quotes in this chapter come from the Shubik paper: *"[t]he game is simplicity itself ... at least two bids have been made"* (109); *"[a] total ... not uncommon"* (110); *"In bargaining ... can be, and are, made"* (111).

25. TRIVIAL: The mathematical sense of 'trivial' does not, however, mean 'easy.' As Richard Feynman described it,

> I still remember a guy sitting on the couch, thinking very hard, and another guy standing in front of him, saying, "And therefore such-and-such is true." "Why is that?" the guy on the couch asks. "It's trivial! It's trivial!" the standing guy says, and he rapidly reels off a series of logical steps ... The guy on the couch is struggling to understand all

this stuff, which goes on at high speed for about fifteen minutes … Finally the standing guy comes out the other end, and the guy on the couch says, "Yeah, yeah. It's trivial."

From "Surely you're joking, Mr. Feynman?," by Richard Feynman, in the segment "A Different Box of Tools." Available on Amazon, and potentially as a free pdf through Google if you search 'richard feynman surely joking pdf' (no quotemarks).

---

The introduction to this book, and significant parts of the first chapter, began life as  a speech I gave in Professor Tamsen Wolff's Public Speaking course. Thanks to Professor Wolff for the excellent and enlightening course.

The cover of this book was adapted from the image *Untitled*, Unidentified Photographer, 1946, released to the commons by the Smithsonian Museum under the *No known copyright restrictions* license. Please contact the publisher immediately if you believe that the image is under copyright in any jurisdiction.

Finally, I'd like to point out that, in the realm of cute economics anecdotes, it's basically impossible to figure out whether you came up with a particular story yourself or if it got planted in your mind at some point by a book or blog. I've done my best to source all my stories but if there are still ideas or examples here that should more properly be credited to another author, please do let me know and I'll be (truly) delighted to make the acknowledgements. Let me pre-emptively confess that any unacknowledged ideas are likely to have come from one of the following sources: Tyler Cowen and Alex Tabarrok at the wonderful

*MarginalRevolution.com*; Andrew Gelman at *AndrewGelman.com*; Jeff Ely at *CheapTalk.org*; Karl Smith at *ModeledBehavior.com*; Steven Landsburg in *The Armchair Economist*; Tim Harford in *The Undercover Economist*; and Thomas Schelling, possibly via the others, because *everyone* owes stories to Thomas Schelling. Other plausible candidates for under-acknowledgment include anyone the above-mentioned bloggers have ever linked to, and my many obscenely-smart friends (though they'll have a harder time proving it — suckers!). I strongly recommend reading any/all of the books and blogs above.

# appendix: sexuality

The models in this book, unless explicitly stated otherwise, apply equally to gay couples and straight couples. The chapters on Signals, Gifts, and Hang-Ups apply exactly-equally to gay and straight relationships; the chapter on Promiscuity includes an explicitly different model for gay relationships because of the different "graph" that exists for same-sex dating. While it's true that I have generally referred to couples in the book as "he" and "she," that's because I ultimately felt I had a choice between writing well and writing in a way that was unmistakably unassuming about gender and sexuality. I did try a number of gender-neutral ways to write various sections, but writing "he-or-she" or making both characters in a single story male or female tended to make it impossible to follow who was who. If you're phenomenally subtle, you'll notice I often used "you and he" or "you and she," which could off course swing in whatever direction you fancy. You are (obviously) more than welcome to mentally flip the genders of one or both characters in almost-all the models with just as much validity.

# acknowledgments

This book got started entirely thanks to Sarah Van Wagenen, one of the kindest and most inspiring people I will ever meet.

Prodigious thanks to Dan Yagudin, for everything and everything, there aren't words to describe.

To Sandra Thomas and Noah Bate, who read my man-u-screept and loved me like a rock.

To Tony Hu, for propitious encouragement and an expert eye in the book's early days.

To Kate Huddleston and Sukrit Silas, for being my Kate and Sukrit.

To Zach Yerushalmi, the most charming man in the world.

To Tao Tao, business legend and patron of the arts.

To Charles and Heidi Blake, my adopted relatives, who laughed at me (and kept me laughing)at all the important moments.

To Ingvill Storoy, for her loveliness and insight; Josh Franklin, for cutting up a chapter and making it infinitely better; Jonny Serfaty, up-and-coming author; and Deborah Chang, for honest goodness.

To my brother Avi, who told me that if I did my best I could someday be somebody's second-best equilibrium solution.

To my brother Avi, who says "I really thought it was Mike who said that, not me, and I discussed this with him. He couldn't remember either. Anyhow, for the record, I certainly would have said it if I'd thought it. And I stand by it, whoever said it."

To Ned Dostaler, for aesthetic guidance.

To James Richardson and Michael Dickman, who taught me how to write.

To Professor Schelling, who I only met once but who changed everything I thought about how to think.

And to my wonderful editor Matthew Halgren, who was so much better to me than I really deserved and believed in me when I'd utterly lost it.

WANT MORE?

visit www.uriwrites.com

contact uri@uriwrites.com

30515660R00047

Made in the USA
Middletown, DE
27 March 2016